QUESTIONING HISTORY

The
American
West

Christine Hatt

A⁺
Smart Apple Media

First published by Hodder Wayland
338 Euston Road, London NW1 3BH, United Kingdom
Hodder Wayland is an imprint of Hodder Children's Books, a division of Hodder Headline Limited.
This edition published under license from Hodder Children's Books. All rights reserved.

Produced for Hodder Wayland by White-Thomson Publishing Ltd.
2/3 St. Andrew's Place, Lewes BN7 1UP, United Kingdom
Copyright © 2004 White-Thomson Publishing Ltd.

Editor: Kelly Davis
Designer: Angie Allison
Consultant: Martin Crawford
Picture researcher: Kelly Davis
Proofreader: Felicity Watts

Published in the United States by Smart Apple Media
2140 Howard Drive West, North Mankato, Minnesota 56003

U.S. publication copyright © 2005 Smart Apple Media
International copyright reserved in all countries. No part of this book may be reproduced in any form
without written permission from the publisher.
Printed in China

Library of Congress Cataloging-in-Publication Data

Hatt, Christine.
The American West / by Christine Hatt.
p. cm. — (Questioning history)
Includes bibliographical references and index.
ISBN 1-58340-443-0
1. West (U.S.)—History—Juvenile literature. I. Title. II. Series.

F591.H286 2004
978'.02—dc22   2003069480

9 8 7 6 5 4 3 2 1

Picture acknowledgements:
Hodder Wayland Picture Library 6 and 60, 32, 61; Mary Evans Picture Library 30, 47, 48; Peter Newark's
American Pictures 4, 7, 8 (from the painting by Harold von Schmidt), 10 (Charles Bird King), 11, 12, 14
(W. H. Jackson), 15 (George Catlin), 16, 17 and *cover* (N. C. Wyeth), 19 (John Gast), 21 and *title page*, 22,
23, 24, 25, 26, 27, 29, 35, 36, 37, 39 (Solomon D. Butcher), 40, 42 (W. Herbert Dunton), 43, 44 and
60/61, 45, 46 (Norman Price), 50 (W. H. Jackson), 51, 53 (Charles Bell), 55, 58, 59; Peter Newark's
Western Americana 31, 41, 49, 54, 57. The maps on pages 20 and 34 were produced by Peter Bull.

CONTENTS

CHAPTER 1
Before 1840 4

CHAPTER 2
Land and People 12

CHAPTER 3
The Great Migration 18

CHAPTER 4
A New Era 32

CHAPTER 5
The End of the Frontier 52

Timeline 60

Glossary 62

Further information 63

Index 64

Before 1840

The American West is usually defined as the area of North America that stretches westward from the Mississippi River to the Pacific Ocean. This huge expanse of land covers about two million square miles (5.2 million sq km) and includes some of Earth's most spectacular landscapes, from shimmering prairie grasslands to snow-covered mountain peaks.

THE FIRST INHABITANTS

The first inhabitants of the West, and all other areas of North and South America, probably began to arrive from Asia about 40,000 years ago. The newcomers then spread slowly across both continents, some groups finding permanent homes, others moving from place to place for thousands of years.

FROM COLONIZATION TO INDEPENDENCE

During the 15th and 16th centuries, men from Spain, France, Britain, and other European lands arrived to claim parts of the

BELOW *The state of North Dakota contains a mixture of typical Western landscapes, from flat, grass-covered prairies to barren areas of eroded rock peaks known as badlands.*

Americas. Most showed little concern for the existing inhabitants, whom they called Indians. Instead, they took over ever-larger areas, Spain becoming the main power in the West. Eventually, though, the British drove out the French, and in the American Revolution (1775–83), Britain's 13 east-coast colonies expelled their British governors. Afterward, the former colonies created an independent country, the United States.

WESTWARD EXPANSION

The citizens of this new land soon began to settle beyond its western border. Then, during the first half of the 19th century, the U.S. government officially acquired more land to the west from Spain and other countries, and this prompted yet more people to move westward. By 1840, large numbers had reached the far edge of Missouri.

Over the next 55 years, westward expansion from Missouri became unstoppable. Attracted first by far-western regions, such as California and Oregon, American-born settlers and immigrants later moved to most areas in between. Farmers, cowboys, gold-miners, railroad-builders, Mormons, freed black slaves, and more all settled in the West for their own reasons. And, as the population steadily grew, sheriffs, soldiers, and the federal (national) government struggled to bring order to this vibrant but often lawless territory.

The West's original inhabitants, the American Indians, suffered greatly as a result of this influx. Gradually, and with government support, the newcomers deprived them of lands where they had lived for generations, and sought to destroy their ancient ways of life. The damaging results of this injustice are still evident.

The dramatic history of the American West has captured the imagination of the world, and tales from its past are told in many films and books. But experts know that the real story is far more complex than anything portrayed in fiction. For this reason, they continue to ask questions about this fascinating region and the people who made it unique.

ABOVE Plymouth colony (see page 7) was founded by British Puritans in search of religious freedom. The Thanksgiving ceremony they introduced when they harvested their first crops in 1621 is still celebrated in the U.S. every year. In this re-enactment, modern Americans wear 17th-century dress.

EXPLORATION AND CONQUEST

In 1492, King Ferdinand and Queen Isabella of Spain paid Italian navigator Christopher Columbus to find a quick sea route to Asia. However, Columbus never reached that continent. Instead, he landed on an island in the Bahamas, off North America. During this and three later trips, he explored more Caribbean islands, as well as parts of Central and South America.

In the 16th century, Spaniards began to colonize the Americas: first, islands such as Cuba, then the mainland. In 1523, Hernán Cortés conquered Mexico's Aztecs, and in 1533, Francisco Pizarro destroyed the Incas of Peru.

Later, in 1565, Spaniards set up the first lasting European colony in North America—St. Augustine, in Florida. The first European settlements in the West were founded in New Mexico in 1598 by another Spaniard, Juan de Oñate. In the 1700s, the Spanish also colonized Texas and California.

FRENCH AND BRITISH COLONIES

By this time, the French had North American colonies, too. In 1608, Samuel de Champlain founded Quebec in modern-day Canada. Then, in 1682, Sieur de La Salle claimed the whole region around the Mississippi River for France, and in 1718, New Orleans was founded at the river mouth.

British colonization centered on North America's east coast. The first lasting British settlement was established in Jamestown, Virginia, in 1607. The second was founded in Plymouth, part of modern Massachusetts, in 1620. Eventually, by 1733, there were 13 British colonies.

In 1756, France and Britain began a war for control of North America, known in Europe as the Seven Years' War and in North America as the French and Indian War. Britain won the conflict in 1763, gaining all former French lands in Canada and east of the Mississippi River, as well as Florida. Meanwhile, Spain won French lands west of the river. Now there were just two major colonial powers left on the continent.

BELOW *This painting shows Samuel de Champlain's first appearance among the Iroquois Indians of Canada.*

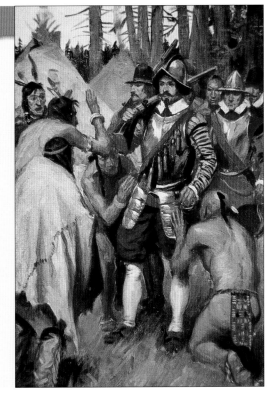

? PEOPLE IN QUESTION

Samuel de Champlain (c. 1570–1635)

Samuel de Champlain was made commandant of all the French territories in North America in 1612. He was a dynamic leader, exploring the region, establishing new settlements, promoting the fur trade, and writing books about his adventures. Some experts have questioned what made him so tireless, suggesting a strong business sense as a possible answer. But de Champlain also claimed to have higher motives: *"By this art [navigation] we obtain a knowledge of different countries, regions, and realms . . . by it the idolatry [worship of idols, or objects that are not true gods] of paganism is overthrown and Christianity proclaimed throughout all the regions of the earth."*

ABOVE *U.S. President*
Thomas Jefferson was fascinated by the West, and after making the Louisiana Purchase (see page 9) he sent an expedition into its vast territories. The expedition leaders, Meriwether Lewis and William Clark (above), left St. Louis in 1804, crossed the Louisiana Purchase, then continued to the Pacific Ocean. They returned safely two years later.

INDEPENDENCE AND AFTER

By the mid-18th century, the loyalty that most Americans in the British colonies had once felt to the monarchy and parliament in London had begun to fade. In addition, almost all the colonists had serious grievances.

First, people objected to British laws that stopped Americans from trading with countries other than Britain. Second, they opposed new taxes designed to make Americans pay for the Seven Years' War. Third, they were angry that Americans were not allowed to settle beyond the Proclamation Line established at the war's end in 1763. To make matters worse, the parliament that introduced these restrictions had no American members.

THE AMERICAN REVOLUTION

In April 1775, fighting broke out between American and British troops. Then, on July 4, 1776, a group of leading Americans issued the Declaration of Independence, which stated that the 13 colonies were now separate from Britain. The fighting continued until 1783, when the Treaty of Paris recognized the United States as a new, independent nation.

After 1783, Americans poured into lands west of the Proclamation Line, and the federal government struggled to control this process (see panel below). But gradually, states such as Kentucky (1792), Tennessee (1796), and Ohio (1803) were created from the new lands.

THE LOUISIANA PURCHASE

Further expansion was hampered by the fact that Louisiana, west of the Mississippi River, was under European control. In 1763, after the Seven Years' War, this land had been granted to Spain. But in 1800, Spain had sold it back to France. In 1803, President Thomas Jefferson persuaded the French to sell the land to the U.S. for just $15 million, doubling the size of the nation.

The U.S. acquired more territory in 1819, when Spain handed over Florida and a small area bordering on Louisiana. The Spanish also abandoned all claims to territory on the Pacific coast north of California, leaving the U.S. free to expand further.

? EVENT IN QUESTION

The 1780s' Land Ordinances: For power or profit?

In 1785, the first law-making body of the U.S., the Continental Congress, introduced the Land Ordinance. It arranged for all land west of the U.S. border to be surveyed and divided into six-square-mile (16 sq km) townships, which were in turn divided into 640-acre (256 ha) plots. The aim was then to sell the plots to settlers for $640 each.

In 1787, Congress also passed the Northwest Ordinance, which dealt specifically with the settlement and government of the large area of western land called the Northwest Territory. It outlined, too, how newly settled regions could become states.

Congress records show the Ordinances were intended to ensure that western settlement was orderly, and that settlers stayed under U.S. government control. But it is also clear that Congress needed to make a profit from the land, as the Revolutionary War had left the U.S. very short of money.

THE AMERICAN INDIAN EXPERIENCE

By the 1790s, the British were still present in lands northwest of the U.S. border. To prevent white Americans from moving in there, they supported resistance by local American Indian peoples—Shawnee, Miami, and Chippewa—who risked losing their ancient territories to the settlers. In 1794, however, U.S. troops defeated the American Indians at the Battle of Fallen Timbers. Afterward, in the 1795 Treaty of Greenville, 11 American Indian peoples surrendered land that would become part of three states, namely Ohio, Indiana, and Illinois.

After the 1803 Louisiana Purchase, U.S. President Thomas Jefferson planned to relocate most American Indians west of the Mississippi River. Faced with such governmental determination, some decided simply to sell their remaining northwestern lands. Shawnee brothers Tenskwatawa and Tecumseh urged all American Indians to recover their pride, but their resistance was almost entirely crushed in 1811 when U.S. troops defeated Tenskwatawa at the Battle of Tippecanoe.

BELOW *Originally named Lalawethika, the Shawnee prophet Tenskwatawa adopted his new name in 1805 after having a vision. Tenskwatawa means "Open Door" and was a sign that he was now open to messages from God.*

THE REMOVAL ACT

The situation for American Indians in the southeast was no better. Some were persuaded to surrender their lands, but the Cherokee, Creek, Choctaw, and Chickasaw refused to budge. Instead, many became farmers and Christians in the hope that the government would let them stay. But the government was under pressure from white settlers who wanted to farm and mine American Indian land.

Tecumseh (1768–1813) and Tenskwatawa (1775–1836)

The Shawnee warrior Tecumseh tried to persuade both northern and southern American Indians that they should join together to fight white Americans. His brother Tenskwatawa, also known as the Prophet, took a more spiritual approach, claiming God had told him that American Indians should reject white ways.

Although the brothers had many followers, their plans failed. Historians who question why suggest several reasons. First, the Americans were determined to eliminate such powerful opponents. Second, the British offered Tecumseh only half-hearted and unreliable support against the Americans. Finally, by his emphasis on unity, Tecumseh angered many traditional American Indian leaders who wanted to act alone, as they had always done.

ABOVE *Tecumseh, Chief of the Shawnee, was killed by American troops led by William Henry Harrison, governor of the Indiana Territory, during the 1813 Battle of the Thames.*

In May 1830, the U.S. Congress passed the Removal Act, which allowed the government to expel American Indians who refused to make their way west voluntarily. Accepting the inevitable, the Choctaw left in 1830, and the Creek in 1832. The Chickasaw were forced out in 1837. Finally, in 1838, U.S. troops rounded up some 18,000 Cherokee and escorted them to Indian Territory (modern Oklahoma). About 4,000 died on this grim six-month trek, now known as the Trail of Tears.

The Removal Act was also used to force more American Indian peoples farther north. In 1832, all their hopes of retaining the northwest ended when the Sauk and Fox peoples of Illinois were driven across the Mississippi.

CHAPTER 2

Land and People

THE GREAT AMERICAN DESERT

By 1840, white Americans had reached the eastern banks of the Mississippi. However, the western regions immediately beyond appeared desolate and earned themselves the name "the Great American Desert" (see panel opposite).

THE GREAT PLAINS

This "Desert" area is largely made up of the Great Plains, which extend about 1,000 miles (1,600 km) west from the Mississippi. Covering about 970,000 square miles (2.5 million sq km), they stretch from Canada in the north to Texas in the south. The eastern two-thirds are mainly flat prairie covered with tall, swaying grasses. Here there is enough rainfall—up to 40 inches (100 cm) annually—to make the soil suitable for farming. However, there

BELOW *Buffalo grazing in North Dakota. In the early 19th century, about 60 million of these creatures lived on the Great Plains.*

are no trees from which settlers could build log cabins, as they commonly did farther to the east. The western third of the Plains, known as the High Plains, is even less hospitable. Here the land rises up to the Rocky Mountains, and only about 10 inches (25 cm) of rain falls. Much of this region is covered with short grasses.

Settlers were deterred as much by Plains weather as by the landscape. In the winter, it is bitterly cold with frequent blizzards, while in the summer, hot, dry periods are interspersed with spectacular thunderstorms and tornadoes. Despite the extreme weather conditions, the 19th-century Plains were still home to huge, roaming herds of buffalo.

THE ROCKIES AND BEYOND

West of the Plains lie the Rocky Mountains, whose peaks and passes were no enticement to settlers. And west of the Rockies are the Great Basin to the south and High Plateau to the north. The Basin is a harsh, desert area, while the Plateau is higher and harsher still, containing the Cascade Mountains and Hell's Canyon, the deepest gorge in the U.S.

"The Great American Desert" was thought to end either where the Plains met the Rockies, or at the western edge of the High Plateau and Great Basin. Either way, the warm lands of western Oregon and California beyond were far more inviting.

? WHAT IF...

Major Stephen Harriman Long had not described the Plains as "the Great American Desert"?

After the 1803 Louisiana Purchase, the U.S. government funded several expeditions into its new territory. One of these expeditions, begun in 1820 and headed by Major Stephen Harriman Long, explored the Great Plains in the region of modern Nebraska and Colorado. Afterward, Long declared that the entire area was *"uninhabitable by a people depending on agriculture"* and coined the term *"Great American Desert."* It was then used on many maps, reinforcing Long's view. The Plains might well have been settled much more quickly if Long's assessment had been different.

THE PLAINS INDIANS

As would-be settlers gazed nervously across the Mississippi, more than 30 American Indian peoples were already living on the Plains. The first to live there had settled on the prairies around the Missouri River by about A.D. 900. They included the Mandan and Hidatsa peoples, who lived in earth lodges.

ABOVE *This 19th-century photograph shows a group of Pawnee Indians outside their earth lodge on the Plains. Unlike the Mandan and Hidatsa, Pawnee lived in lodges only during the winter. During summer buffalo hunts, they sheltered in tepees instead.*

The women of these peoples farmed the fertile, river-valley land where their lodges stood, growing crops such as maize and squashes. At some times of the year, men helped them with tasks such as weeding. But in the summer, the men left their villages to hunt buffalo, whose meat could be eaten fresh or preserved for the winter. These American Indians also ate many wild plants, and used them as medicines.

HIGH PLAINS HUNTERS

The starkly beautiful but arid western plains were home to other peoples such as the Lakota and Cheyenne. These High Plains Indians lived in tepees, buffalo-hide tents, that had patterns or animals painted on them to ward off bad luck. Unlike lodges, tepees were portable, so that their nomadic inhabitants could carry their homes with them.

Indian life on the High Plains depended entirely on the buffalo, whose flesh was eaten and whose hides were used for tepees,

Did smallpox drive some American Indians to the High Plains?

After Europeans arrived in the Americas, millions of native people died from diseases that the newcomers brought, as they had no immunity to them. Smallpox killed many Hidatsa and Mandan Indians. In the 1837 outbreak, for instance, Mandan numbers fell from 1,600 to 125.

Smallpox also had an impact on American Indians who did not catch it. In the 18th century, peoples such as the Lakota were heading west, and some began to live as settled farmers like the Mandan. But soon after smallpox struck, they left for the High Plains. Experts think fear of the disease was partly responsible, but so, too, was the arrival of horses, which made the American Indians more mobile and able to survive as nomadic buffalo-hunters in a more hostile environment.

clothes, and more. Men originally killed these beasts by covering themselves in wolfskins, crawling in among them, then firing arrows from their bows, or by stampeding them over a cliff. But hunting changed in the 18th century, after horses began to reach the Plains from South America, where they had been imported by the Spanish. The speed and mobility of horses made them ideal for hunting, and by the 19th century, Plains Indians were accustomed to both hunting and fighting their enemies on horseback.

BELOW *Lakota Indians hunting buffalo on horseback. George Catlin, who painted this picture in 1835, recorded many scenes of 19th-century American Indian life.*

ABOVE *The 19th-century Shoshoni chief Washakie. Once they had horses, some Shoshoni occasionally traveled to the Plains to hunt buffalo. The name Washakie means "Shoots-the-Buffalo-Running."*

THE GREAT BASIN

The high, dry deserts of the Great Basin were home to three main peoples—the Paiute, Ute, and Shoshoni. Here, American Indians gathered edible plants, and caught fish and animals such as jackrabbits and lizards.

Only the Ute and some Shoshoni adopted the horse from Europeans, but all the Basin Indians lived nomadically. In winter they sheltered in caves, and in summer built wickiups (huts made of wood and brush).

THE HIGH PLATEAU

More American Indian peoples lived among the canyons of the High Plateau, including the Cayuse and Nez Percé. They relied mainly on fish for food, but they also hunted deer and gathered plants such as the camas lily. In winter, Plateau peoples lived in sunken pit houses, while in summer they built large reed lodges.

Following European contact, both the Cayuse and Nez Percé became successful breeders and traders of horses. But the Cayuse were later hit by European diseases, and eventually dispersed.

CALIFORNIA

Not all Indians of the West lived in "the Great American Desert." More than 50 peoples inhabited California, some along the Pacific coast, such as the Pomo, others inland, such as the Miwok. The Spanish were the first Europeans to come into contact with the California Indians, soon forcing them to become Roman Catholic

Christians and work for missions. After the region came into U.S. hands, the Indians fared little better (see pages 52 and 53).

THE SOUTHWEST

The red desert landscape of the Southwest was home to two distinct groups of American Indians. The first were Pueblo peoples such as the Hopi, who had inhabited the region since at least 1200. They lived in multistory adobe houses and grew crops such as maize. The Navajo and Apache had arrived from the north much later, probably in the 15th century. Both enthusiastically adopted the horse and became expert hunters and warriors. They also clashed ferociously with white Americans and their Pueblo Indian neighbors.

? PEOPLE IN QUESTION

Sacagawea (c.1787–1812)

Sacagawea was a Shoshoni woman who married Toussaint Charbonneau, a French fur trader. The couple was hired by Lewis and Clark when they made their 1804–06 expedition across North America (see pages 8 and 9). Sacagawea acted as interpreter and guide, but historians now question whether it was her status as a woman and mother or an Indian that contributed most to the expedition's success.

BELOW *In this painting, Sacagawea guides the explorers Lewis and Clark on their 1804–06 expedition.*

Clark certainly thought her female status helped, as this extract from his journals shows:

"The Wife of Shabono [Charbonneau] ... We find reconciles all the Indians, as to our friendly intentions. A woman with a party of men is a token of peace."

CHAPTER 3

The Great Migration

DEPRESSION AND DYNAMISM

Around 1840, several factors combined to usher in a new era of westward expansion across North America. Among them was the serious economic depression that hit the U.S. in 1837, causing bankruptcies and unemployment. Against this background, the possibility of a fresh start in the West looked decidedly appealing.

Also in the 1840s, a new spirit of optimism spread among some sections of the U.S. population. This was the era of "Young America," a movement made up of politicians, economists, and writers who believed that the U.S. was on the brink of greatness and should not be held back by old-fashioned European ways. Money was there to be made, business to be done, and western land, to which the U.S. as yet had no right, was there to be settled.

PRESIDENT POLK

In 1844, James Knox Polk, a member of the Democratic Party, was elected U.S. president, and the next year was sworn into office. Polk agreed with many of the Young America movement's ideals, especially expansionism. In particular, he aimed to extend the U.S. into Texas, then under Mexican rule, and into Oregon, north of California, which was jointly controlled by the U.S. and Britain (see pages 20 through 23).

In July 1845, as the campaign for annexation of these territories (joining them to the U.S.) grew stronger, one journalist coined a phrase that seemed to capture white Americans' view of their role exactly. In *The United States Magazine and Democratic Review*, John L. O'Sullivan criticized foreign governments who objected to U.S. expansion into Texas, explaining that it was "the fulfillment of our manifest destiny to overspread the continent allotted by Providence for the free development of our yearly multiplying millions." Armed with the arresting catchphrase "manifest destiny,"

and the conviction that Providence (God) was on their side, Polk and his followers now defiantly faced the opposition they knew must come.

ABOVE *In this 1872 painting, "manifest destiny" is personified as a woman moving purposefully westward across the U.S.*

 PEOPLE IN QUESTION

Jim Beckwourth (c. 1800–66)

Some Americans waited for neither government approval nor the company of friends and family before heading west. These were the mountain men, who made their living by buying and selling furs. Among them was former black slave Jim Beckwourth. At first, he worked for General William Henry Ashley, founder of the Rocky Mountain Fur Company. But later he went his own way and was adopted by Crow Indians. Beckwourth claimed to have persuaded the Crow chief that he was his long-lost son. But historians are not sure whether this story is anything more than a tall tale!

THE OREGON QUESTION

Thanks to President Polk's determination, by the mid-19th century the boundaries of the U.S. reached the Pacific coast.

The dispute over the Oregon country (which was far larger than the modern state of the same name) was resolved first. In 1818, the U.S. and Britain had agreed that they should jointly occupy the territory, but by 1845 about 6,000 Americans had settled there, and were urging Polk to make it part of the U.S. He demanded the whole region, but in 1846, after harsh negotiations, he secured a smaller area, with a coastal detour to the south that allowed Britain to keep all of Vancouver Island.

BELOW *This simplified map shows how the U.S. expanded westward during the 19th century.*

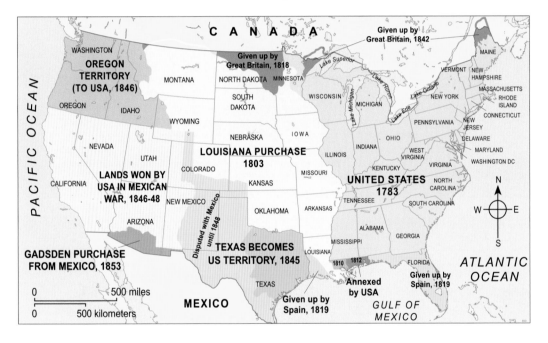

TROUBLE IN TEXAS

U.S. claims to Texas were not so easily settled. In 1821, Spain had granted independence to its American colonies. From then on, Mexico had ruled these lands, stretching from California in the west to Texas in the east.

To encourage the development of Texas, Mexico let U.S. farmers settle there. In return, it required them to adopt Mexican citizenship and Roman Catholicism, but they refused to conform. As a result, fighting broke out in 1835. Finally, on April 21, 1836, at San Jacinto, a Texan force led by Sam Houston crushed the

Mexicans. Texas then became independent, and Houston was elected president.

THE MEXICAN WAR

Houston wanted Texas to become a U.S. state, and in 1845, President Polk admitted it into the Union. But the Mexicans thought the Texan borders extended too far west, including land that was rightly theirs. Polk supported the Texan claim, and so the Mexican War began in 1846. American forces slowly gained the upper hand, and in 1848 ended the conflict by capturing Mexico City. In the peace treaty, the Texans' interpretation of their borders was confirmed, and Mexico granted California and vast lands in the southwest to the U.S.

ABOVE One event from the 1835–36 war between Texas and Mexico is remembered above all others. This is the Battle of the Alamo, which took place on March 6, 1836, at the Texan fortress of the same name. There, 187 Texans, including an already famous fighter named Davy Crockett (shown here using his rifle as a club), bravely but unsuccessfully resisted an attack by several thousand Mexicans.

? EVENT IN QUESTION

The annexation of Texas: A pro-slavery plot?

Texan Americans angered the Mexicans by keeping black slaves, in defiance of Mexican law. At this time, the slavery question was causing severe tension in the U.S., with Southern states supporting its continuation and Northern states pressing to stop its expansion west.

The plan to annex Texas was first proposed by a Southerner, President John Tyler. Tyler claimed that if the U.S. failed to annex Texas, anti-slavery Britain would intervene, paying Texas to ban slavery, then campaigning for abolition across the South. Many Congress members thought Tyler's tactics were simply a pro-slavery plot designed to make fearful Southerners support his wish to annex Texas as a slave state. Many modern experts also think Tyler's claims were mere propaganda.

MEN AND WOMEN WITH A MISSION

The lush lands of Oregon and California were the first to tempt large numbers of Americans west. Among the first to head there were Christian missionaries eager to spread their faith among the American Indians. Their dreams of mass conversion were seldom realized, however. Often Indians clung to their existing spiritual beliefs, wanting only to learn how to farm or use guns. And sometimes misunderstanding led to tragedy. For instance, in 1847, two missionaries, Marcus and Narcissa Whitman, were killed by Cayuse Indians who were angry that more Cayuse than Americans were dying in a measles outbreak. The real reason for the many deaths was Indian lack of immunity, but the Cayuse had believed that Marcus, a doctor, was killing them.

ABOVE *Marcus Whitman, the American medical missionary who was killed by Cayuse Indians in Oregon in 1847. Marcus's wife, Narcissa, and her friend Eliza Spaulding were the first white American women to reach the West.*

ON THE TRAIL

Of the 350,000 or so people who crossed North America between 1840 and 1870, however, most were ordinary men, women, and children who thought they could build a better life in the West. Poor economic conditions in the East supported this belief (see pages 18 and 19), while descriptions contained in early migrants' letters of the hot climate and flourishing crops in California and Oregon's Willamette Valley also attracted them.

Most of these migrants traveled along two routes that missionaries had followed before them, known as the Oregon and California Trails. Both routes usually began on the banks of the Missouri River, then followed the North Platte River over the Plains. Next, the trails crossed the Rocky Mountains and continued together until they reached Fort Hall. Here, people heading for California went south and Oregon-bound travelers north. This hazardous journey of about 2,400 miles (3,900 km) usually took six months.

The decision to emigrate: A man's or a woman's choice?

Many women who headed west in the 19th century kept diaries. They often say that the decision to leave family and friends in the East was made by their husband, and that they went mainly because they believed it was their Christian duty to support their spouse. Some experts accept these reports at face value. In *Women and Men on the Overland Trail* (1979), for example, John M. Faragher writes:

"Not one wife initiated the idea [of leaving]; it was always the husband. Less than a quarter of the women writers recorded agreeing. . . ."

But others, such as Julie Roy Jeffrey in *Frontier Women: The Trans-Mississippi West, 1840–60* (1979), take a different view:

"Whatever ideology had to say about the necessity of female submission, women felt free to disrupt the male emigration project and . . . had bargaining powers."

BELOW *A map of the old Oregon Trail.*

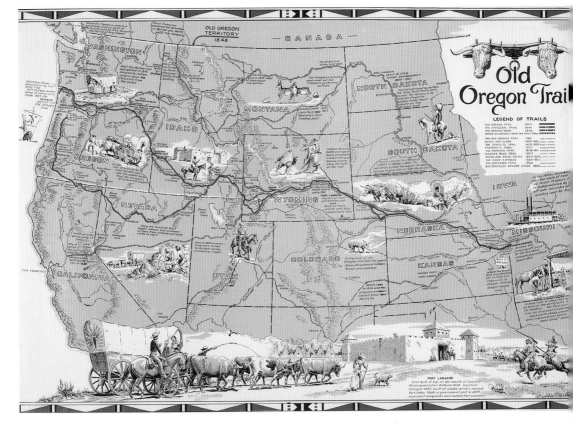

WESTERN WAGONS

As emigration to the West increased, long processions of covered wagons began to cross the Plains. At first, emigrants often traveled in Conestoga wagons, which had wooden bodies that sloped out at either end like ships' hulls, and canvas covers stretched over iron hoops. But Conestogas were up to 26 feet (8 m) long, and often needed eight horses or oxen to pull them. As a result, they were impractical for the long trek across prairie and mountain.

In time, most overlanders began to use either smaller versions of the boat-shaped Conestogas or strengthened, compact farm wagons with straight sides and covers. These were not only far easier to maneuver, but they could also be pulled by just two animals.

GETTING READY

From the 1840s, people could buy guidebooks that told them how to prepare for their journey. These books advised emigrants to buy many items in addition to their wagon and animals, including repair tools, rifles and ammunition, cooking pots, food, and sturdy clothing. The total cost could be as much as $1,000, and people often sold most of their possessions to finance the trip. The aim was to be ready in the spring so that the journey would be over before winter snows started to fall.

BELOW *A pioneer woman collects buffalo chips (droppings) in Kansas during the 1880s. The chips were used as fuel for heating and cooking.*

LIFE ON THE PIONEER TRAIL

Days on the trail were long, with adults rising at 4 A.M. Men spent their time driving the wagons, looking after the animals, and hunting buffalo to provide meat for their families. Women built cooking fires using buffalo chips (droppings), prepared meals, washed clothes, and cared for children. About one-fifth of female overlanders also gave birth on the trail.

The wagons were halted at dusk, then arranged in a circle around a central fire. After the evening meal, adults slept in the wagons and children in tents outside.

ABOVE *Wagons formed protective circles at Independence Rock, beside the Sweetwater River, a landmark on the Oregon Trail.*

DEATH AND DANGER

Many overlanders feared American Indian attacks, but these were quite rare. Instead, cholera, typhoid, and measles posed the worst threats—about 9,500 emigrants died of these and other diseases. Accidents such as drowning and falling under the wheels of moving wagons also killed many, while some people simply failed to cross the Rockies before winter and perished in the snow.

? EVENT IN QUESTION

American Indian attacks

Experts have long questioned how frequent American Indian raids on wagon trains really were. In his book *The Plains Across: The Overland Emigrants and the Trans-Mississippi West, 1840–1860* (1979), John D. Unruh Jr. provided answers based on careful research. His conclusion was that during those years only 400 of a total 250,000 emigrants were killed by Indians, and most were not attacked at all.

ABOVE *In this mid-19th-century scene, Mormon pioneer families pull hand-carts on the long journey to Salt Lake City.*

MORMON MIGRATION

In the 1820s, an American farm boy named Joseph Smith claimed to see visions that told him to found a new church true to the teachings of Jesus Christ. Then in 1830, he published *The Book of Mormon* and founded The Church of Jesus Christ of Latter-day Saints. It soon had hundreds of members, but more enemies, many of them traditional Christians who rejected Mormon ideas. Smith therefore decided to base his church in the West, where he hoped followers would be free to believe as they chose.

A NEW LEADER

The Mormons settled first in Ohio, then Missouri, but were driven out. Finally they moved to Illinois. Here, Smith soon angered traditional Christians and some Mormons by introducing controversial new doctrines and practicing polygamy (taking several wives). Eventually he was jailed after a riot, and on June 27, 1844, a mob broke in and shot him dead.

? EVENT IN QUESTION

The Mountain Meadows Massacre

In 1857, a group of emigrants from Missouri and Arkansas were making their way along the Oregon Trail. As they crossed Deseret, they taunted the Mormons there, a few Missourians even claiming to have killed Joseph Smith. In revenge, the Mormons helped Paiute Indians attack the wagon train at a place called Mountain Meadows. Between them, the two groups killed about 130 people.

Historians do not question the basic facts of this massacre, but do argue about Brigham Young's attitude towards it. There is no evidence that he ordered the attack. However, he did not condemn it. He also ordered the victims' memorial to be pulled down.

A farmer named Brigham Young replaced Smith and soon decided to lead his followers to the far West. So, in 1846, he and 12,000 others set out for the Great Salt Lake Valley. On July 24, 1847, the first 148 arrivals, including Young, founded Salt Lake City. It became the heart of Mormon territory, which they called the State of Deseret.

ABOVE *Brigham Young, photographed in 1851.*

SUCCESS AND CONFLICT

The Mormons were industrious, making crops thrive in their arid lands. But in 1848, after the Mexican War, their territory passed from Mexican to U.S. control, and U.S. laws banned polygamy, which was now common practice among Mormon men.

Thinking only force would make Mormons submit, U.S. President James Buchanan sent troops west in 1857, but a non-violent settlement was reached. In return for a pardon for their previous disobedience, Mormons agreed to keep the law. And, in 1896, Mormon lands joined the U.S. as the state of Utah.

GOLD!

A discovery made in California's American River on January 24, 1848, led to the rapid transformation of large areas of the West. On this day, James Marshall, a foreman on the California estate of a rich man named John Sutter, went to examine the estate's new sawmill, located on the riverbank. There he noticed something glinting under the water—and found it was gold.

News of the find spread, and many more people came to the mill site. They included Mormon Sam Brannan, who set up a shop nearby that stocked goldmining tools. To increase his sales, he went to San Francisco, then a Spanish-Mexican village of about 800 people, and paraded along the street, shouting "Gold! Gold! Gold from the American River!"

THE RUSH BEGINS

Now the news spread like wildfire. Soon thousands were making their way to California—from the eastern states, and from South America, Europe, China, Australia, and many other countries. In 1849, the flow of migrants increased further, and San Francisco was soon home to about 35,000 people.

Around 92 percent of the "forty-niners," as the newcomers became known, were men. Many were single, but others left behind wives, children, and steady jobs. Not all spent their days mining. Some decided a safer income could be earned by running shops, banks, and other businesses that the immigrants needed. Many of the women who caught "gold fever" made their money by cooking meals, washing laundry, and running hotels for men.

A NEW CALIFORNIA

The rapid influx of people brought many changes to California. Settlers soon established a rough form of local government, but they also pressured the federal (national) government to make the territory a state. It did so in 1850, banning slavery there, as the thousands of new Californians did not want to lose their jobs to unpaid slaves. Wealthy investors and new industries were also attracted to the state as a result of the increased population.

? EVENT IN QUESTION

Were American goldminers racist?

Relations between American and foreign miners were often uneasy, and the Chinese, in particular, were barely tolerated. In 1850, California's state government passed a law making all foreign miners pay a monthly tax of $20. This forced many out, but the Chinese stayed—by 1852, 25,000 lived there. In 1882, the Chinese Exclusion Act, a national law, banned immigration from China for 10 years.

Historians can find no legitimate reason why the Chinese were so despised. Often white miners were angry simply because the Chinese found gold in mines that they had abandoned. However, the real reason may have been racism. One politician of the time described the Chinese as an *"Oriental octopus [that] corrupts morals. . . ."*

BELOW *This engraving shows Chinese miners trying their luck in the gold fields of California in 1849. The man in the foreground is using a cradle (see page 30) to help him.*

MINING CAMPS

Goldmining camps sprang up in many places, but especially beside rivers, in whose waters gold could be found. Early camps usually contained just a few makeshift shelters, such as log cabins, canvas tents, or brushwood shacks. In this environment, hygiene was poor and rats were common.

THE QUEST FOR GOLD

Miners spent almost all their time looking for gold. At first they used a technique called placer mining. This involved scooping up river gravel with a metal pan, then rinsing it so that any heavy gold particles it contained quickly separated out and sank. Larger gravel samples were placed in wooden troughs called cradles. Water was then poured through the cradles as they were rocked, again encouraging gold to sink.

Once a miner had some gold, he took it to an assay office. Here it was tested (assayed) to check its authenticity, and to see what impurities it contained. Finally, the gold was given a value, and the miner was paid. When river gold was still easy to find, many miners earned about $500 a day, the equivalent of nine months' ordinary wages. But few made the life-changing discoveries of their dreams.

CHANGING TIMES

The easily accessible river gold soon ran out, and by the 1850s, the only ways to reach more were to crush surface rocks or dig underground using heavy equipment. Such equipment was too costly for ordinary people, so mining corporations moved in. Some California miners took corporation jobs, but others moved on to new gold sites such as Pikes Peak, Colorado, where a major find was made in 1859.

ABOVE *A miner pans for river gold in the American West.*

? EVENT IN QUESTION

The fate of the California Indians: Avoidable or inevitable?

In 1845, there were 150,000 American Indians in California, but the gold seekers brought diseases such as cholera that struck them hard. Ancient Indian buffalo-hunting grounds were also destroyed by wagons and mines, making food scarce. Worse still, many gold hunters deliberately killed Indians so that by 1856, there were only 25,000.

Experts now question whether the federal government could have done more to prevent this tragedy. Federal officials working in California did try to save some land for local Indian peoples. But, under pressure from miners who wanted the right to dig for gold everywhere, the U.S. Senate in Washington overruled them. Yet national politicians knew what was happening in the West, as shown by an 1850 government report: *"The majority of the [California] tribes are kept in constant fear on account of the . . . inhumane massacre of their people. . . . They become alarmed at the . . . flood of immigration which spreads over their country. . . ."*

31

CHAPTER 4

A New Era

THE AMERICAN CIVIL WAR

All the Northern states of the U.S. were moving toward the abolition of slavery by 1804. But, by the 1850s, the Southern states were still grimly resisting change.

Westward expansion increased the tension, as Southerners and Northerners argued about whether each new state should be slave-holding or free. Trouble flared again in 1854, when politicians organized Kansas and Nebraska into territories, with a view to making them states. According to an 1850 agreement, both states would be free. But, to avoid Southern objections, the Kansas-Nebraska Act (1854) said inhabitants should have the right to vote on the question.

This well-meaning compromise was disastrous, as slavery supporters from neighboring Missouri voted in Kansas, ensuring the election of a pro-slavery territorial government. Anti-slavery Free Soilers, who formed most of the population, then appointed a rival legislature, and a minor guerrilla war began. Hundreds died, causing the territory to become known as Bleeding Kansas.

BELOW *An engraving dating from 1866 (a year after slavery was finally abolished across the U.S.), questioning whether slavery is really dead.*

CIVIL WAR AND THE WEST

Civil War finally broke out between the North and the South in 1861. The Southern states, known as the Confederacy, at first planned to seize the West. Confederate troops from Texas were therefore sent to New Mexico to begin the conquest. But in the 1862 Battle of Glorietta Pass, Union (Northern) troops, led by Colonel John M. Chivington, drove them decisively back.

Kansas, meanwhile, had become a free state in 1861. In 1863, pro-slavery Confederates led an attack on the Free Soiler stronghold of Lawrence, Kansas, killing about 180 men. However, two years later, the war ended in victory for the anti-slavery Union.

NAVAJO AND CHEYENNE

In 1863, U.S. troops forced the Navajo Indians of Arizona and New Mexico out of their lands, murdering many in the process. The next year, survivors were forced to make the "Long Walk" to a grim and distant reservation in a place called Bosque Redondo.

Many High Plains Cheyenne also met a tragic fate in 1864. They had begun to clash with settlers, but in the fall of that year, they met with white officials to negotiate peace. Afterward, they returned to their camp in Sand Creek, Colorado. There, on November 29, Chivington and his troops massacred at least 200 of them.

? PEOPLE IN QUESTION

John M. Chivington (1821–94)

Born in Ohio, John M. Chivington became a Methodist minister and preached against slavery. In the Civil War, Chivington led the anti-slavery Union forces at Glorietta Pass in 1862. But he also massacred the Cheyenne at Sand Creek two years later, having earlier stated:
"Cheyennes will have to be . . . completely wiped out . . . before they will be quiet. . . . the only thing to do is kill them."

How could a man so opposed to slavery treat American Indians so shockingly? Historians suggest his political ambitions were the likely reason. Chivington hoped to represent Colorado in the U.S. Congress and may have thought he could win votes by taking an anti-Indian stance. In fact, the Sand Creek Massacre ruined his reputation for good.

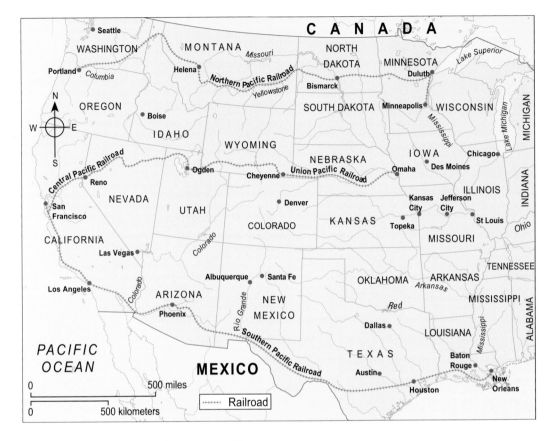

ABOVE *This map shows the three main railroads built across the West during the 19th century.*

ACROSS THE CONTINENT

By 1860, there were railroads in every state east of the Mississippi River, but trains crossed very little of the West. However, as the Western economy developed, the federal government saw the need for a railroad that would carry goods between the East and the West. Plans took shape in the 1850s, but there were delays as the estimated costs were huge, and Northerners and Southerners could not agree on a route.

Just before the Civil War, most Southern states broke away from the U.S., so Congress was able to push through its railroad plans without their consent. In 1862, it passed the Pacific Railroad Act, allowing construction of a cross-country track.

CONSTRUCTION AND CONFLICT

The Central Pacific Railroad Company built the new track east from California, while the Union Pacific Railroad built west from Nebraska. Work began at both sites in 1863.

? **WHAT IF...**

The railroad had never reached the West?

The railroad brought great benefits to the West. It obviously provided a far quicker means of transportation (for both goods and people) than horses, stagecoaches, or canal boats. The railroad also encouraged new towns to grow up along its route, and new businesses to thrive.

However, the railroad's arrival had costs, too. Cheap imports brought from the East by train caused business failures and job losses. And more lasting harm was done to the American Indians, whose lands were divided, and whose traditional prey, the buffalo, were shot by the building crews and the professional hunters who came after them.

If the railroad had never reached the West, fewer people would have settled there, local industry would probably not have flourished, and the region might not have become so fully a part of the U.S. More positively, the region's Indians might have been able to maintain some of their old ways of life.

The Central Pacific had to cut through the solid granite of the Sierra Nevada Mountains. Some 6,000 Chinese men blasted out the rock, about 1,200 of them dying in the process. In the East, 10,000 Irish and other laborers laid track across the Plains much faster, but faced fierce opposition from Indian peoples. Eventually, the tracks met in Utah, and on May 10, 1869, the two railroad presidents hammered in a golden spike to signal the completion of the work.

This success prompted construction of other railroads into the West. They included the Northern Pacific, which ran from Minnesota to Oregon, and the Southern Pacific, which eventually stretched from California to Louisiana. Both opened in 1883.

BELOW *Chinese railroad workers building a bridge on the western slope of the Sierra Nevada Mountains in 1867.*

THE HOMESTEAD ACT

The federal government passed the 1862 Homestead Act to encourage people to settle on and farm more Western territory, including "the Great American Desert." The terms of the act were simple—the state would give anyone who was over 21 or the head of a family 160 acres (64 ha) in return for $10 and a commitment to cultivate the land for at least five years. This offer was open not only to existing U.S. citizens, but also to anyone who had applied for citizenship.

Most of those who accepted the proposal already had farms in the Midwest. But the offer was also publicized in Europe, and thousands of new immigrants poured in from countries such as Sweden and Germany. By 1900, almost 600,000 land claims had been made under the provisions of the Homestead Act.

PROBLEMS AND SOLUTIONS

In the 1870s, the usually dry Plains experienced high rainfall, so

BELOW *Swedish immigrant settlers in the late 19th century. Like thousands of others, they were attracted by the popular belief that working the land would improve the climate. This was expressed in the common saying "rain follows the plow."*

many new settlers produced a good harvest. As a result, a myth arose that farming itself encouraged wet weather. This belief enticed more people to the West, but the truth was very different. The Plains was an extremely harsh environment in which to farm, and water was generally scarce. What is more, 160 acres (64 ha) of Plains land rarely provided a decent living.

Over time, the government addressed these concerns. In 1873, for example, it passed the Timber Culture Act, which let settlers have an extra 160 acres (64 ha) if they planted trees on at least a quarter of them. Later, in 1877, the Desert Land Act came into force. It allowed settlers to claim low-cost, 640-acre (256 ha) grants in desert areas, as long as they introduced irrigation. But by 1890, despite these measures, more than 65 percent of homesteaders had not turned their land into profitable farms.

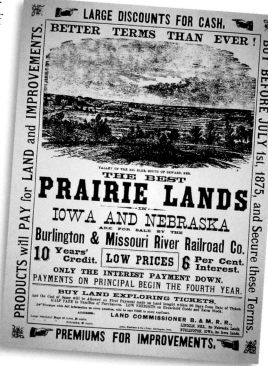

ABOVE *Federal and state governments granted huge areas of land to railroad companies to encourage them to build across the West. The companies then sold their land cheaply to settlers, bringing thousands to the region. This poster is advertising land owned by the Burlington and Missouri River Railroad Company.*

? PEOPLE IN QUESTION

Speculators: Good or bad?

Wealthy speculators, who bought land cheap and then sold it later at a much higher price, had operated in the West since the early days of settlement. The Homestead, Timber Culture, and Desert Land Acts, designed to help ordinary settlers, also gave these men more chances to acquire Western land at low cost. They usually snapped up the best-watered areas, then advertised them for sale in newspapers.

At the time, the speculators were very unpopular. But, by purchasing large amounts of land, they did help to open up the West, and to attract rich settlers. Some of these settlers had money to invest in new businesses, and created wealth and jobs for others. Without intending to do so, speculators may therefore have benefited the West as a whole rather than just themselves.

SLAVERY AND AFTER

When the Civil War ended in 1865, a highly significant change was made to the U.S. constitution. This was the Thirteenth Amendment, which outlawed slavery throughout the country. Despite having lost the war, the Southern states were reluctant to accept this new state of affairs, so federal troops were stationed there to ensure that they did not deny black people their rights. However, long before the last troops left, in 1877, Southerners began to use both state laws and violence to do exactly that.

EXODUSTERS

Against this background, some black people in the South decided to move West, and became known as Exodusters. This was a reference to the Bible story about the exodus (departure) of the Hebrews from slavery in Egypt.

The preferred destination for many was Kansas, and one of the first black settlements there was Singleton Colony. From there, former slave Benjamin "Pap" Singleton issued an invitation to other black people living in the East to "Come and join us in the promised land!"

The largest black settlement, however, was Nicodemus, near the Solomon River. About 300 blacks from Kentucky moved there in 1877, paying $5 each for the privilege, and it was finally home to around 700.

Within three years of the troop withdrawal from the South, there were about 15,000 Exodusters in the West, farming some 20,000 acres (8,000 ha). Most experienced racism there, just as they had in the Southern states, but white hostility was usually less severe. Black farmers' other main difficulty was making the dry Plains earth produce crops, and women often took a second job, such as housecleaning, to make ends meet.

? EVENT IN QUESTION

The black exodus to the West: Right or wrong?

The first black people in North America, a group of 20, were brought there by a Dutch sea captain in 1619. As time passed, thousands more were shipped across the Atlantic Ocean from West Africa to serve whites as farm and domestic slaves. Treated simply as property by their white owners, slaves suffered great cruelty. Eventually, however, public pressure combined with economic and political changes to bring abolition, first in the Northern states of the U.S., then, after the Civil War, in the Southern states as well.

The westward flight of the Exodusters to avoid continuing racism in the South was supported by many black leaders. But others, including ex-slave Booker T. Washington, felt it was an admission of defeat. In 1881, Washington set up the Tuskegee Institute in Alabama, where black people could learn manual trades. He firmly believed blacks should work in their home states, and encouraged would-be Exodusters to "cast your bucket down where you are."

BELOW *The Shore family, African-American homesteaders, at their house in Nebraska, in 1887.*

HOMESTEAD HOMES

Extreme weather of all kinds hit the Plains, so it was essential for new arrivals to build a shelter quickly. Many constructed sod houses, commonly known as "soddies." They were made of large pieces of turf and had holes for windows, so they had the advantage of being cheap. But they leaked badly in wet weather and were often infested with insects.

ANIMALS AND CROPS

Homesteaders usually kept a few cows to pull plows and provide milk, and chickens for meat and eggs. But most of their time was spent growing crops such as wheat. This was hard in the Plains' arid soil, so farmers paid drillers to locate underground water, then used wind-pumps to bring it to the surface.

New items of farm equipment were widely adopted on the Plains. They ranged from a plow invented in the 1830s, whose steel moldboard did not get stuck in the thick soil, to a mechanized harvester, introduced in 1878, that could both cut cereal crops and tie them into bundles. Following its invention in 1874, barbed wire was much used, too, as it was a cheap way of dividing up the land.

ABOVE *An 1881 advertisement for Glidden's Patent Barbed Wire. Joseph Glidden was a major barbed wire manufacturer.*

PLAINS PROBLEMS

Despite such improvements, there were some grim aspects of life on the Plains. Chief among them was the weather (see also pages 12 and 13). Homesteaders endured freezing temperatures in the winter, and blazing heat, thunderstorms, and prairie fires in the summer. The hot months also brought huge swarms of grasshoppers, which ate the crops without mercy.

Loneliness was another problem, as homesteads were often many miles apart. However, traveling preachers, known as circuit riders, visited regularly, and the arrival of the railroad made it easier for people to meet, too.

? EVENT IN QUESTION

The development of Plains agriculture

Farmers from different countries and different parts of the U.S. all brought their own agricultural techniques to the Plains. But did they farm exactly as they had done in their homelands? Or did they adapt to the special conditions of the West?

According to specialist historians, most groups began by farming in the way that they already knew, but amended their practices when it was sensible to do so. For example, Russians started by growing wheat, as they had back in Russia. They even imported seeds for the varieties of wheat they preferred, such as "Turkey Red." But it soon became clear that, in the West, maize was a highly profitable crop, so they began to grow that as well.

CATTLE RANCHING

Almost all the techniques and traditions now associated with cattle ranching in the American West (see also pages 44 and 45) developed in Mexico and New Mexico when they were under Spanish control. Here the first cowboys, known as *vaqueros*, kept cattle on open ranges (land not divided into fields by wooden fences or wire), caught them with lassos, branded them with their owners' marks, and drove them to market for sale.

It was not until the 1860s, after the Civil War, that large-scale, Mexican-style ranching arrived in the U.S. In the chaos of the war years, Spanish Criollo cows that had crossed into Texas interbred with English and American cattle to produce Texas Longhorns. By the war's end, millions of these hardy creatures were roaming wild. And someone saw the chance to make money.

BELOW *Mexican vaqueros rounding up Texas Longhorns. American butchers unkindly described these scrawny animals as "8 pounds of hamburger on 800 pounds of bone and horn."*

FROM TRAIL TO RAIL

There were so many cows in Texas at the end of the war that each one was worth $4 at the most. But in Eastern cities, such as New York, a good animal fetched up to $80. Any Texan could, therefore, see that it would be better to sell his cattle in the East. The only question was how to get them there.

The man who solved this problem was Joseph G. McCoy. By then, railroads had reached the West, but none ran as far south as Texas. So he suggested driving cattle north to railheads (depots), then loading them onto trains for the journey east. McCoy tried out his plan in 1867, and it was a huge success. Soon cowboys were guiding thousands of steers (male calves to be sold for meat) along cattle trails every spring.

LIFE ON THE CATTLE TRAIL

Up to 5,000 cattle were driven along a trail at one time. The trail boss led the herd from the front. Other cowboys rode on both sides and at the back to stop cattle from escaping. Drives usually covered about 15 miles (25 km) a day and faced many dangers, from stampedes to rustlers. But cowboys looked forward to partying at the end of the trail in "cow towns" such as Abilene, Kansas.

ABOVE *Joseph G. McCoy, the cattle dealer who in 1867 established Abilene, Kansas, as the first "cow town."*

? PEOPLE IN QUESTION

Joseph G. McCoy (1837–1915)

McCoy, a shrewd businessman from Illinois, liked to claim that he was the first person to work out how to get Texas cattle to Eastern cities. Historians say that he was certainly determined, talking to several railroad company bosses before the owner of the Hannibal and St. Joseph Railroad agreed to his plan. However, several other entrepreneurs had the same idea. McCoy was just lucky enough to find the right business partner.

RANCH LIFE

When they were not on the trail, most cowboys lived on a ranch. The central point of any ranch was the ranch house, where the owner lived. It was often a timber building, but in the southwest, ranch houses were made of adobe (sun-dried mud bricks).

Cowboys lived in the bunkhouse. This was usually a cramped timber hut, where up to 10 men slept and spent their leisure hours. Favorite pastimes included playing dice, checkers, and dominoes, and making rope for catching cattle by weaving together strips of leather, horsehair, or plant fibers.

On some ranches, cowboys cooked in the bunkhouse. On others, they used a separate messhouse. The food they prepared usually came from the ranch, as they preferred fresh meat, eggs, and milk to shop-bought items, which they called "States food."

BELOW *Cowboys bathing in a water hole during the 1880s.*

THE WORKING DAY

Cowboys fed and nursed cattle, and ensured that they stayed inside the ranch by patrolling its borders. In the spring, as the drive

? PEOPLE IN QUESTION

Cowboys

Films and books generally depict cowboys as handsome, strong, white men. But historians have found that at least one in seven cowboys were black. About 1 in 10 were Mexican, and their language, Spanish, was more widely used among cowboys than English.

There are many other myths about cowboys. In particular, they were not as fit as is often suggested. Life in the saddle was so harsh that they often developed rheumatism, misshapen spines, and bow legs.

approached, they had to round up the steers and bring them to the ranch, an operation that took several days and was led by a man called the round-up captain. Next, they caught new calves and burned the ranch's brand into their hides with a hot iron. Only then could the herd move north.

ABOVE *A cowboy trail boss in Montana, in 1888. A lasso and other tools of his trade are attached to his saddle.*

HORSES

A cowboy needed a good horse. In fact, most cowboys had several, each one skilled in a different task. For example, some horses were good at separating steers from a herd, a process known as cutting. Others were ideal for riding when cowboys were trying to rope cattle (that is, to catch them with a lasso).

CLOTHES

Cowboys prided themselves on their special clothing. Favorite items included brimmed hats, which kept the sun out of their eyes, and bandannas (neckerchiefs), which kept the dust out of their mouths. Cowboys also wore woolen trousers or jeans, and chaps (leather leggings that fit over the top). Their outfits were completed with heeled leather boots that gripped their stirrups.

FRONTIER TOWNS

Towns grew up in all sorts of places in the American West. For instance, some were built along transportation routes, some developed from ramshackle goldmining camps, and some grew up at the railheads where the long cattle trails ended. At first, many towns were just a rough collection of buildings, usually including a trading post. But as they grew, most were laid out in a strict grid pattern, with ruler-straight streets.

ABOVE *This painting shows a sight that was familiar in many Western towns—a Wells, Fargo and Company stagecoach in front of a local company office.*

Another common feature of frontier towns was their exceptionally wide roads. A distance of 80 feet (24 m) from side to side was quite usual, but in the town of Omaha, Nebraska, founded in 1854, the streets were 100 feet (30 m) across. These wide roads allowed space for wagons and stagecoaches to turn around easily. They were also a sign that Western planners liked to think big. One European visitor noted: "Every town in the West is laid out on a plan as vast as though it were destined . . . to contain a million of inhabitants."

BUILDINGS AND BUSINESSES

Every Western town of any size contained churches, schools, banks, stores, and post offices, as well as saloon bars where weary miners, cowboys, and others could spend their non-working

hours. Many towns also had a newspaper that printed stories of local interest—the silver-mining settlement of Tombstone, Arizona, for example, produced a journal called the *Tombstone Nugget*. Sheriffs' offices and courthouses were also common features of these settlements.

Two of the most famous names in the West appeared on many frontier town shopfronts, too. Wells, Fargo and Company was founded in 1852 to provide banking services for miners. In time, it also ran a successful stagecoach service. The service provided by Western Union was also extremely popular. People who wanted to contact someone elsewhere in the U.S. simply went to a Western Union office and handed over their message to a tele-graph operator, who would send it for them.

? PEOPLE IN QUESTION

Medicine men

Medical care in the West was very basic, and most people treated everything from malaria to the common cold themselves. In such circumstances, it was easy for "medicine men," offering so-called miracle cures, to do good business. These characters were regular visitors to frontier towns, where they loudly proclaimed the benefits of potions such as "Dr. Sherman's Pricklyash Bitters." At the time, they managed to deceive a great many people. The modern assessment is that the great majority were simply con artists selling nothing but colored and flavored water.

LAW AND ORDER

The law was difficult to enforce in the wild, open spaces of the West, which was exactly why thousands of criminals went there. Many were former soldiers who had fought on the Confederate (Southern) side in the Civil War, then drifted into crime. Among them were Jesse James and his gang, who held up 5 stagecoaches, 7 trains, and 12 banks between 1866 and 1882.

RIGHT A poster advertising a $500 reward for the arrest and conviction of Jesse James. One of the other main bandits in Jesse's gang was his brother, Frank.

Solitary gunfighters were also active in the West. The most notorious was John Wesley Hardin, the son of a preacher. His first victim was an ex-slave, and the next three were the soldiers who tried to arrest him for this crime. Before he was finally arrested in 1874, Hardin killed more than 20 men—but he still opened a law office after his release.

LAW ENFORCEMENT

Before official lawmen and courts reached the West, people set up their own vigilante committees to catch criminals. There were more than 200 of these committees in the region, and they punished offenders harshly—public hangings were common.

Once established, the law system was quite complex. U.S. marshals had responsibility for law enforcement in an entire state. Next came sheriffs, with authority over a state subdivision known as a county. Town marshals, meanwhile, were responsible for prevention and detection of crime in their own towns or other settlements.

Law courts were also introduced into the West, and trial by jury gradually replaced vigilantism. But some early judges sentenced criminals according to their own whims rather than government rules. For example, Judge Roy Bean, who held his court in a Texas saloon bar, liked to punish outlaws by sending them into the desert without food, water, or weapons.

ABOVE Belle Starr was the adopted name of Myra Belle Shirley, a farmer's daughter. She became an outlaw early in life and was particularly notorious for rustling (stealing) horses and cattle. Her exploits earned her another name, the "Bandit Queen."

? PEOPLE IN QUESTION

Wyatt Earp (1848–1929)

Wyatt Earp was a law officer, first in Kansas, then in Arizona, where he served as a U.S. marshal. Nevertheless, he spent much of his time gambling and took care to befriend rich local businessmen, investing heavily in mines and land.

Earp is now best remembered for his part in a Tombstone shoot-out. In the years beforehand, cowboys had regularly visited the town to steal and kill. Earp's business friends had therefore asked him, his brothers, and his friend Doc Holliday to hunt down the men involved. In 1881, the two groups met at the OK Corral, where three of the cowboys were shot dead. However, historians question Earp's role in this conflict. In their view, it was not a straight fight between the lawless and law-abiding, but a struggle between landless cowboys and powerful business interests.

ABOVE *Fort Laramie, Wyoming in the 19th century. The fort is now a National Historic Site open to visitors.*

SOLDIERS ON THE FRONTIER

Once people began to head west in large numbers, they asked for protection from Indian attacks. The federal government's response was to send troops to the region occasionally, as a show of strength. However, it soon became clear that permanent military bases were necessary, so in 1846, Congress agreed to build forts there. One of the first, Fort Laramie, in Wyoming, was an old fur-trading post built in 1834. It was taken over and extended by the army in 1849.

By the 1850s, the West contained 79 U.S. Army posts, although some were only small camps. The full-size forts were huge structures—Fort Laramie, for example, contained 22 separate buildings, including barracks, stables, a hospital, and officers' quarters. But life for the ordinary soldiers who lived inside these sprawling military posts was often depressing. Poor pay, harsh punishments for even minor acts of disobedience, and an unchanging diet of dry hardtack biscuits and meat (both often crawling with maggots), all contributed to high levels of desertion.

? PEOPLE IN QUESTION

Buffalo soldiers

Four regiments of black soldiers served in the West—two infantry and the 9th and 10th Cavalry. Cheyenne Indians called them "buffalo soldiers" because their tightly curled hair looked like the fur between a buffalo's horns.

Black soldiers had to endure dreadful racism. They were not allowed to lead themselves, but had to serve under white officers, and were often given the worst equipment and slowest horses. Historians now ask why any black man would join the army under such circumstances. They suggest that, first, black people suffered racism everywhere, so the situation in the army was no different. And, second, a soldier's job was better than many others available to blacks, providing some status and security, as well as regular pay and a place to live.

ABOVE *Henry O. Flipper, the first black graduate of West Point Military Academy. He served with the 10th U.S. Cavalry.*

THE CIVIL WAR AND AFTER

During the Civil War, many soldiers left the West to fight in the battles raging across the East. But the forts were still manned, some troops participating in the violent actions against the Navajo, Cheyenne, and other Indians that occurred during these years (see page 33). After the war, many of the original soldiers returned, as there were few other jobs available. They were joined by new recruits, including large numbers of recent immigrants who did not speak English and so found it hard to understand orders.

From the 1860s to the 1890s, clashes between the federal government and the Indians grew more serious. As a result, the cavalry units based in Western forts regularly had to intervene, eventually crushing the Indian resistance (see pages 52 through 55).

CHAPTER 5

The End of the Frontier

THE INDIAN WARS

As more and more overlanders reached the West in the 1840s and 1850s, the Plains Indians grew increasingly hostile. The federal government, therefore, decided it would have to formulate a clear Indian policy that would maintain peace but not obstruct white settlement. But, under the circumstances, peace was not possible.

The government's first significant attempt to deal with the problem since the 1830 Removal Act (see page 10) came in 1851. In that year, Lakota, Cheyenne, and other Indians met federal officials at Fort Laramie and reluctantly agreed to live and hunt within fixed boundaries. In return, they were to receive annual donations of goods, such as farm tools, from the government.

The policy was never likely to hold and did not. Most Indians had no interest in becoming settled farmers and simply returned to their traditional hunting grounds. Meanwhile, white settlers happily trespassed on Indian territory if it contained something that they wanted. A major gold discovery in Pikes Peak, Colorado, for example, was made on Cheyenne land. Eventually, tensions between settlers and the Cheyenne ran so high that they led to the 1864 massacre at Sand Creek (see page 33).

DIFFERENT VIEWS

Broadly speaking, white people in the West believed that Indians should be confined in fixed areas, while Easterners thought they should be educated, baptized, and assimilated into white society. The Sand Creek massacre heightened these differences and led to Eastern demands for a more humane approach. So, in 1867, the government offered the Cheyenne, Kiowa, and Comanche new lands. Some agreed to move, but serious bad feeling remained.

THE PEACE COMMISSION

Trouble also flared among the Lakota during the 1860s, after a new route from Colorado to the Montana goldmines, called the

Bozeman Trail, was built across their territory. In revenge, a group of Lakota killed U.S. Army captain William J. Fetterman, and 80 men under his command, during an ambush in 1866.

This incident led to further demands for change, so in 1867, the federal government formed the Peace Commission. During a meeting at Fort Laramie in 1868, it negotiated an end to the war with the Lakota. And it also proposed that all the Plains Indian peoples should move to two "reservations" of land set aside for their use, one in the north of the region and one in the south.

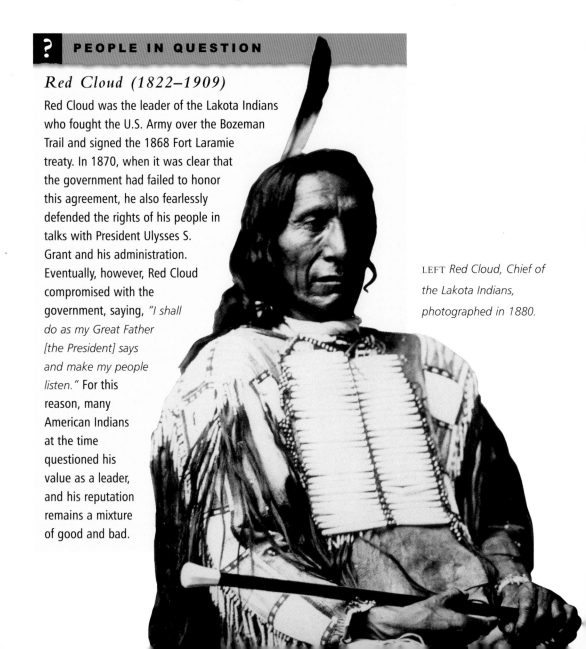

? PEOPLE IN QUESTION

Red Cloud (1822–1909)

Red Cloud was the leader of the Lakota Indians who fought the U.S. Army over the Bozeman Trail and signed the 1868 Fort Laramie treaty. In 1870, when it was clear that the government had failed to honor this agreement, he also fearlessly defended the rights of his people in talks with President Ulysses S. Grant and his administration. Eventually, however, Red Cloud compromised with the government, saying, *"I shall do as my Great Father [the President] says and make my people listen."* For this reason, many American Indians at the time questioned his value as a leader, and his reputation remains a mixture of good and bad.

LEFT *Red Cloud, Chief of the Lakota Indians, photographed in 1880.*

THE END OF THE BUFFALO

Settlers had always killed buffalo for meat. But from the 1870s, they slaughtered these beasts in the thousands. The plan was not only to sell the hides, but also to speed up the decline of the Indians by exterminating the animal on which they depended for food. From 1870 to 1883, professional hunters, including the infamous "Buffalo Bill" (William Cody), shot more than 40 million.

Some Indians tried to stop the killing. From 1874 to 1875, Kiowa, Comanche, Cheyenne, and others attacked hunters in Texas during a conflict called the Red River War. Eventually, the army intervened to destroy all the Indians' possessions, leaving the men with no choice but to settle on reservations.

LITTLE BIGHORN AND WOUNDED KNEE

The Lakota, meanwhile, were fighting miners in the Black Hills of South Dakota. The army responded by sending in troops led by Lieutenant Colonel George Armstrong Custer, who on June 25, 1876, attacked them and their leaders Crazy Horse and Sitting Bull beside Montana's Little Bighorn River. The Indian band was 2,500 strong, while Custer had just over 600 men. He and his immediate command of 272 men were all killed in what became known as Custer's Last Stand.

Despite this victory, most Lakota were forced onto a reservation. But some began to take part in rituals known as Ghost Dances, which they thought would restore their old ways of life. In a clash with troops over the dances, Sitting Bull was killed, so his followers fled to another leader, Big

BELOW *Buffalo Bill was not only a hunter and soldier but also an entertainer. In his "Wild West Show," he and his fellow performers acted out famous battles and other events from Western history.*

Foot. In 1890, soldiers made them camp at Wounded Knee Creek, South Dakota. There, on December 29, they were massacred, and the dream of rebirth died.

Other Indian peoples met with equal failure. In 1877, Chief Joseph of the Nez Percé Indians led his followers on a 1,200-mile (1,900 km) trek to Canada, but the army forced them to surrender.

ABOVE *The Apache chief Geronimo resisted reservation life for years, but in 1886, he had to give up his bitter struggle. He is shown here (far right) with two of his warriors in the Arizona desert.*

THE DAWES ACT

By this time, the government had decided its reservation policy was wrong, as it encouraged the continuation of Indian culture. So, in 1887, it passed the Dawes Act, which promoted the break-up of reservations by offering plots of land to individual Indians. They received 47 million acres (19 million ha), but almost double that amount was sold to white settlers. In 1889, the old Indian Territory was opened up to whites—it would become the state of Oklahoma.

? **EVENT IN QUESTION**

American Indian policy

Historians who question why the federal government's Indian policy changed so much over time do not provide flattering answers. White politicians often claimed that they wanted to "civilize" American Indians and make them a part of white society. But the real reason was often greed—they simply wanted the Indians' land and the valuable metals and other minerals on that land. Racism was a powerful factor, too. Few white people considered American Indians equals, with the same rights over their lives and property as whites enjoyed.

CHANGE ON THE RANGE

The cowboys' way of life died along with the Indians'. As more homesteaders arrived, they divided the land into fields, often using barbed wire, so cowboys could no longer herd animals over the open range. As a result, cattle drives became increasingly difficult, and arguments between cowboys and farmers more frequent.

Other changes had an equally significant impact. After Gustavus Swift invented the refrigerated railroad car in 1881, it was no longer necessary to transport live cattle to the East. Cattle were therefore killed and butchered in the West. As both refrigerated cars and slaughterhouses were expensive, but profits were high, rich businessmen began to invest in the cattle industry, introducing changes which were resented by the cowboys.

MOVING NORTH

The arrival of homesteaders (see pages 36 and 37) on southern ranges encouraged many ranchers to move cattle north into states such as Wyoming, Montana, and North and South Dakota during the 1880s. There, large areas of open range were still available, so traditional round-ups and drives could continue. However, the ranges grew steadily more crowded as increasing numbers of cattle were moved there.

The next blow to traditional ranching was struck by the weather. During the winter of 1886 to 1887, the temperature plummeted. Cattle were weighed down by thick layers of ice, and often could not escape the snows because their feet were stuck in the ice, or they were fenced in by barbed wire. Hundreds of thousands did not survive these cruel months, which cowboys and ranchers called "The Great Die-Up."

NEW BEGINNINGS

After this tragedy, investors who were not cattlemen at heart simply abandoned the ranges. Many of the remaining ranchers reduced the size of their herds, fenced them in, and began to grow crops as well. Sheep farming also became popular, leading to fights between sheep and cattle owners who both claimed the same grazing land.

The range wars

The great cattle barons of the northern ranges were often backed by rich investors. Cowboys hated the changes introduced by the barons, and homesteaders usually supported the cowboys. In many places, such as Johnson County, Wyoming, this clash of cultures led to violence, with cowboys stealing cattle from the barons, and investors hiring gunmen to attack the cowboys. According to some historians, these "range wars" were not simple feuds between cowboys and cattle barons. Instead, they were struggles between profit-driven big businessmen who wanted to incorporate the West into the economy of the East, and ordinary people who valued traditional ways of life. The investors finally defeated the cowboys across much of the West.

At the end of the 19th century, another threat to cowboy life emerged. Oil was found on the Texas plains, and a new industry was born.

BELOW *Cowboys in Johnson County, Wyoming, 1892. Cowboys in this region, angered by investors' power and pride, began to steal their cattle. In response, the investors hired gunfighters to kill the rustlers. However, the gunmen managed to shoot only two cowboys dead before they were stopped by a group of ordinary citizens and had to be rescued by the U.S. cavalry.*

ABOVE *Anna Webb of Kansas, a rancher's daughter, photographed in the 1880s. Many women like her played a significant part in settling and developing the West.*

CHANGING VIEWS

Between 1840 and 1895, the American West was transformed. White settlers had arrived to stay, the Indians had retreated, and the federal government had extended its grip across the U.S. to the Pacific Ocean.

Until the late 20th century, the story of the West was told mainly from the white settlers' point of view. Their progress across the North American continent was seen as the result of superiority and strong character, and the fate of the Indians as an inevitable consequence. In addition, the exploration of the West was told as a story of male achievement and ability, with the participation of women largely ignored or downplayed.

In recent years, this view has been widely rejected. Now, experts point out that the West's uniqueness was created not only by white people of European origin, though they of course played their part, but also by the Mexicans and Spaniards who lived in California long before they arrived, by the black Exodusters who settled in Kansas, by the Chinese who built the railroad, and by the men and women from all over the world who mined for gold. Above all, they point to the contributions of the American Indian peoples, who were the West's first inhabitants.

WOMEN IN THE WEST

The role of women has also been reassessed. Most overlanders traveled westward in family groups, and many would not have survived without the hard work undertaken by the women in their parties. Likewise, many women, newly free of the ladylike behavior expected in the East, played full parts in running their Western farms.

THE WEST TODAY

Since the late 19th century, the West has seen more great changes, from the rise of the Los Angeles-based film and Texas-based oil industries to the establishment of national parks and the growth of tourism. American Indians have also made serious attempts to rebuild their traditions. Meanwhile, people from many countries are still settling in the West so that it continues to change and grow.

ABOVE *Nat Love, an African-American cowboy, photographed in the 1870s. For many years, black people's contribution to Western economy and culture was scarcely recognized.*

? PEOPLE IN QUESTION

Frederick Jackson Turner (1861–1932)

In 1890, a U.S. government report declared that white settlement had advanced so far west, the country no longer had a true frontier. Wisconsin University historian Frederick Jackson Turner responded to this statement by writing an essay called "The Significance of the Frontier in American History." Published in 1893, it claimed that the frontier and settlers' efforts to push it westward had created Americans' unique character, which in his opinion was self-reliant, individualistic, and inventive.

   Modern historians question Turner's interpretation. Most accept that settlers were hardy and resourceful—they had to be. But experts also point out that these farmers were not always individualistic, as co-operation was necessary to survive. And, above all, historians query Turner's wider argument that the frontier was *"the meeting point between savagery and civilization,"* now preferring to emphasize that there was savagery and civilization on both sides.

Timeline

1492
Christopher Columbus reaches the Americas.

1565
Spaniards found St. Augustine, Florida.

1598
Spaniard Juan de Oñate founds first European colonies in the West, in New Mexico.

1607
British found their first lasting North American settlement in Jamestown, Virginia.

1608
French explorer Samuel de Champlain founds the settlement of Quebec, Canada.

1620
British Puritans found colony of Plymouth in the area of modern Massachusetts.

1682
Sieur de La Salle claims region around the Mississippi River for France.

1700s
Spaniards colonize Texas and California.

1756–1763
Seven Years' War between Britain and France for control of North America; Britain wins.

1775–1783
The American Revolution; Britain's 13 American colonies win their independence and the U.S. is founded.

1794
U.S. troops defeat American Indians in northwestern territories at Battle of Fallen Timbers.

1803
Louisiana Purchase of North American land from France doubles the size of the U.S.

1804–1806
Meriwether Lewis and William Clark cross the West to reach the Pacific.

1811
American troops defeat American Indians at Tippecanoe.

1819
The U.S. gains Florida and other North American land from Spain.

1820
Major Stephen Harriman Long explores land acquired in the Louisiana Purchase.

1821
Spain grants independence to colonies in the Americas; colonies then ruled by Mexico.

1830
Removal Act allows U.S. government to relocate American Indians in western lands.
Joseph Smith founds The Church of Jesus Christ of Latter-day Saints.

1835–1836
Texas wins its independence from Mexico.

1837
Economic depression hits the U.S.

1838
18,000 Cherokee Indians follow "Trail of Tears."

1840s
White settlement reaches eastern banks of Mississippi.

1844
James Polk elected president.

1845
President Polk admits Texas into the U.S. as a state.

1846
New Mormon leader Brigham Young begins the trek to the West with his followers.

1846–1848
War between Mexico and the U.S.; the U.S. wins.

1847
Mormons found Salt Lake City.

1848
James Marshall discovers gold in California's American River.

1850
California joins the U.S.

1851
Fort Laramie Treaty; Indians agree to live and hunt within fixed boundaries.

1861–1865
Southern and Northern states fight American Civil War; Northern states win.

1862
Battle of Glorietta Pass: Southern troops driven out of West.
Homestead Act passed.
Pacific Railroad Act passed.

1864
U.S. troops massacre Cheyenne Indians at Sand Creek.

1865
Thirteenth Amendment to U.S. Constitution bans slavery throughout the U.S.

1869
Central Pacific and Union Pacific Railroads complete rail track across the West.

1870s
White hunters kill millions of buffalo on the Plains.

1874–1875
Kiowa, Comanche, and Cheyenne Indians fight Red River War against buffalo hunters in Texas; Indians eventually forced to settle on reservations.

1876
June 25: Custer and U.S. troops defeated by Lakota Indians at the Battle of Little Bighorn.

1877
Nez Percé Indian leader Chief Joseph leads followers to Canada, but U.S. troops defeat them.
Exoduster settlement founded in Nicodemus, Kansas.

1882
Chinese Exclusion Act.

1883
Northern Pacific and Southern Pacific Railroads open in the West.

1887
Dawes Act passed.

1889
Former Indian Territory, now known as Oklahoma, is opened up to white settlement.

1890
U.S. troops massacre Lakota Indians at Wounded Knee, South Dakota.
U.S. census declares white settlement has extended so far west that the U.S. no longer has a frontier.

1892
Johnson County War between cattle barons and cowboys.

1896
Mormon lands become part of the U.S. as the state of Utah.

Glossary

adobe Brick made of mud or clay that is dried hard in the sun.

capitalism An economic system in which individuals, rather than the state, own businesses and run them mainly for personal profit.

cholera A serious disease of the intestines that causes severe stomach pain and diarrhea. People usually catch it by eating infected food or drinking infected water.

colony A country or other territory that is ruled by the government of another state.

Confederacy The collective name given to the 11 states of the American South that left the U.S. in 1861, then fought the Northern states in the American Civil War. The Confederate states rejoined the U.S. after losing the war in 1865.

Congress The law-making body of the U.S. It is made up of two houses, the Senate and the House of Representatives.

Democratic Party A major U.S. political party. It became very popular in the early 19th century, when it was believed to represent the views of ordinary people.

Free Soilers People whose aim was to stop the spread of slavery into new U.S. territories. They founded the Free Soil Party in 1848, but later many joined the more influential Republican Party, founded in 1854. It also opposed the expansion of slavery.

hardtack Hard, square, cracker-like biscuits made of wheat.

homestead A house and the adjoining land used for farming, particularly a house and land settled as a result of the 1862 Homestead Act. About 1.4 million homesteads were established in the American West between 1862 and 1920.

Indian Territory The territory that the 1830 Indian Removal Act set aside for permanent settlement by Indians who had been forced from their homes in the southeastern U.S.

Covering most of modern Oklahoma, as well as some other areas, the Territory was soon settled by whites as well as Indians.

irrigation The supply of water to land by various means, such as digging canals that allow river water to flow across the soil.

land grant A land transfer made to a private citizen or company by the U.S. government. Between 1860 and 1900, about 500 million acres (200 million ha) of western land was distributed, much of it for the establishment of homesteads and the building of railroads.

Midwest The states that make up the wide, north-central section of the U.S. It is usually considered to stretch from Ohio in the East to Colorado in the West.

mission A building set up by a church in which to teach people about the Christian faith and to hold services. When Spain ruled the American West, the Roman Catholic Church set up many missions there and tried to convert local Indians to Christianity.

mountain man One of the many adventurous men who caught beavers and other animals in the Rocky Mountains, then sold them for their furs. Mountain men were particularly active from 1810 to 1840, before there was widespread settlement in the West.

paganism Religious faith that involves the worship of many gods and often does not have fixed beliefs written down in holy books.

pit house A type of winter home built by Indians of the High Plateau. Pit houses consisted of large, circular pits dug down into the earth with wooden roofs on the top. People climbed into them through a hole in the roof.

polygamy The practice, common especially among early Mormons, of having several wives at the same time.

railhead The station or stopping place on a railway track where a cattle drive ended.

Further information

range war An armed conflict between wealthy cattle barons and ordinary cowboys. Range wars were so-called because they took place on the range (that is, the open land where cattle were kept).

reservation An area of land that the U.S. government set aside for settlement by American Indians. The process of forcing Indians onto reservations began in the eastern states during the late 18th century, but it reached its high point in the West about 100 years later.

sagebrush A tall plant with spiky, grey-green leaves that grows in the Great Plains, the Great Basin, and other Western areas. Sagebrush bushes are often about two feet (.5 m) tall, but can grow to twice the size of a man.

sawmill A building where people operate machines that cut wood.

Senate One of the two houses that make up Congress (see previous page).

telegraph A fast means of communication that involves sending electrical signals along wires. Telegraph messages were usually sent in Morse code (that is, groups of short or long sounds each representing a particular letter or number).

typhoid A serious disease that causes fever and a deep pink rash. People usually catch it by eating infected food or drinking infected water.

Union The U.S. considered as a collection of states joined together under one national government.

vigilante A person who sets out to enforce law and order, but who is not appointed by a government or other authority. In the American West, groups of vigilantes often caught and punished supposed criminals without giving them a fair trial.

BOOKS

Cox, Clinton. *Forgotten Heroes: The Story of the Buffalo Soldiers.* New York: Scholastic, 1996.

Seymour, Flora W. *Sacagawea: American Pathfinder.* New York: Simon & Schuster Children's, 1991.

Sullivan, George E. *Lewis and Clark.* New York: Scholastic, 2000.

Wadsworth, Ginger. *Words West: Voices of Young Pioneers.* New York: Houghton Mifflin, 2003.

NOTE ON SOURCES

A source is information about the past. Sources can take many forms, from books, films, and documents to physical objects and sound recordings.

There are two types of sources, primary and secondary. Primary sources date from around the time being studied; secondary sources, such as this book, have been produced since that time. In general, primary sources are more accurate but contain much narrower information than secondary sources.

Here are some guidelines to bear in mind when approaching a written or drawn primary source:
1. Who produced it and why?
2. When exactly was the source produced?
3. Might the source have been altered by an editor, censor, or translator?
4. Where was the source produced? Which country, town, region, etc.?
5. Does the source tie in with other sources you have met, primary and secondary?
6. Where has the source come from? Has it been selected by someone else, or did you find it through your own research?

Index

Numbers in **bold** refer
to pictures.

African-American homesteaders
 38, 39, **39**
Alamo, Battle of the **21**
American Civil War 32, 33, 51, 61
American Indians 5, 10, **10**, 11,
 11, 14, **14**, 15, **15**, 16, **16**, 17, **17**,
 25, 31, 52, 53, **53**, 54, 55, **55**,
 58, 59
American Revolution 5, 8
Apache **55**

barbed wire 41, **41**, 56
Britain 4, 5, 7, 8, 10
buffalo 12, **12**, 13, 14, **15**, 54
Buffalo Bill 54, **54**

cattle ranching 42, **42**, 44, 45
Chinese Exclusion Act 29
Chinese immigrants 29, **29**, 35, **35**
Christianity 7, 10, 17
Clark, William **8**, 17
Columbus, Christopher 6
cowboys 5, 42, 43, 44, **44**, 45, **45**,
 56, 57, **57**, **59**
Crazy Horse 54
Custer, Lieutenant Colonel
 George Armstrong 54

Dawes Act 55, 61
de Champlain, Samuel 7, **7**
Declaration of Independence 8

Earp, Wyatt 49
Exodusters *see* African-American
 homesteaders

Fallen Timbers, Battle of 10, 60
Fort Laramie 50, **50**

France 4, 5, 7, 9
frontier towns 46

Geronimo **55**
Glorietta Pass, Battle of 32
gold 28
goldminers 5, 29, **29**, 30, **30**, 31, **31**
Great Plains 12

Homestead Act 36
homesteaders 36, **36**, 37, 38, 39,
 39, 40, **40**, 41, 56, 57
horses 15, **15**, **44**, 45, **45**
Houston, Sam 20, 21

Indian Wars 52

James, Jesse 48, **48**
Jefferson, Thomas 8, 9, 10

Lakota 15, **15**, 52, 53, **53**, 54, 55
Land Ordinances 9
law and order 48, 49
Lewis, Meriwether **8**, 17
Little Bighorn, Battle of 54
Louisiana Purchase 9, 10, 13

McCoy, Joseph G. 43, **43**
medicine men 47
Mexican War 21
missionaries 22, **22**
Mormons 5, 26, **26**, 27, **27**

oil 57, 59
Oregon Trail 23, **23**
overlanders 22, 23, 24, **24**, 25, **25**

Pawnee **14**
Peace Commission 52, 53
Plymouth **6**, 60
Polk, James Knox 18, 19, 20, 21

Proclamation Line 8, 9
Puritans **6**

racism 29, 39, 51, 55
railroads 34, **34**, 35, **35**
range wars 57, **57**
Red Cloud 53, **53**
refrigeration 56
Removal Act 10, 11
reservations 53, 54, 55
Rocky Mountains 13, 22

Sacagawea 17, **17**
Sand Creek Massacre 33, 52
settlers *see* homesteaders
Seven Years' War 7, 8
sheep farming 56
Sitting Bull 54
slavery, abolition of 32, **32**, 38, 39
slaves 5, 21, 39
smallpox 15
Smith, Joseph 26
soldiers 50, 51, **51**
Spain 4, 5, 6, 7, 9
stagecoaches **46**, 47

Tecumseh 10, 11, **11**
Tenskwatawa 10, **10**, 11
Thanksgiving **6**
Tippecanoe 10
Trail of Tears 11
Treaty of Greenville 10
Treaty of Paris 9

wagons 24, 25, **25**
Washington, Booker T. 39
Western Union 47, 47
women 23, 24, **24**, 49, 58, 59
Wounded Knee 54, 55

Young, Brigham 27, **27**